The Beechworth Bakery Bears

as heard by frank prem

To Tom and all the staff at the Beechworth Bakery
From a grateful early-morning pre-work coffee drinker

Published by Wild Arancini Press
Title: *The Beechworth Bakery Bears*
ISBN: 978-1-925963-09-0 (p-bk)
ISBN: 978-1-925963-12-0 (h-bk)

Copyright © 2020 Frank Prem

All rights reserved:
No part of this publication may be reproduced, stored in a retrieval system, or transmitted in any form or by any means, electronic, mechanical, photocopying, recording or otherwise, without prior written permission from the publisher and author.

Cover Design by Frank Prem and Leanne Murphy

smile

everybody *smi-ile*

come on *smi-ile*

we've got a job
to do

smile
for our *visitors!*

maybe
one of us
will go *home* with them!
so

smi-ile
smile now

everybody

smi-ile

speaking on behalf of . . .

hello?

hello?

who
um . . .
who is doing the . . .

me
me
look at me
I can do it

let *me* speak

ple-ease

where? here!

             (hee hee)

                              hee hee
                              they don't know
                              where we are

                              hee hee

                              we
                              are *here!*

listen up

listen carefully

Tom is telling us
what we must do

he is telling us
how we must
behave

and he is telling us
there'll be
a cup of tea

and honey

at the end
of another
working day

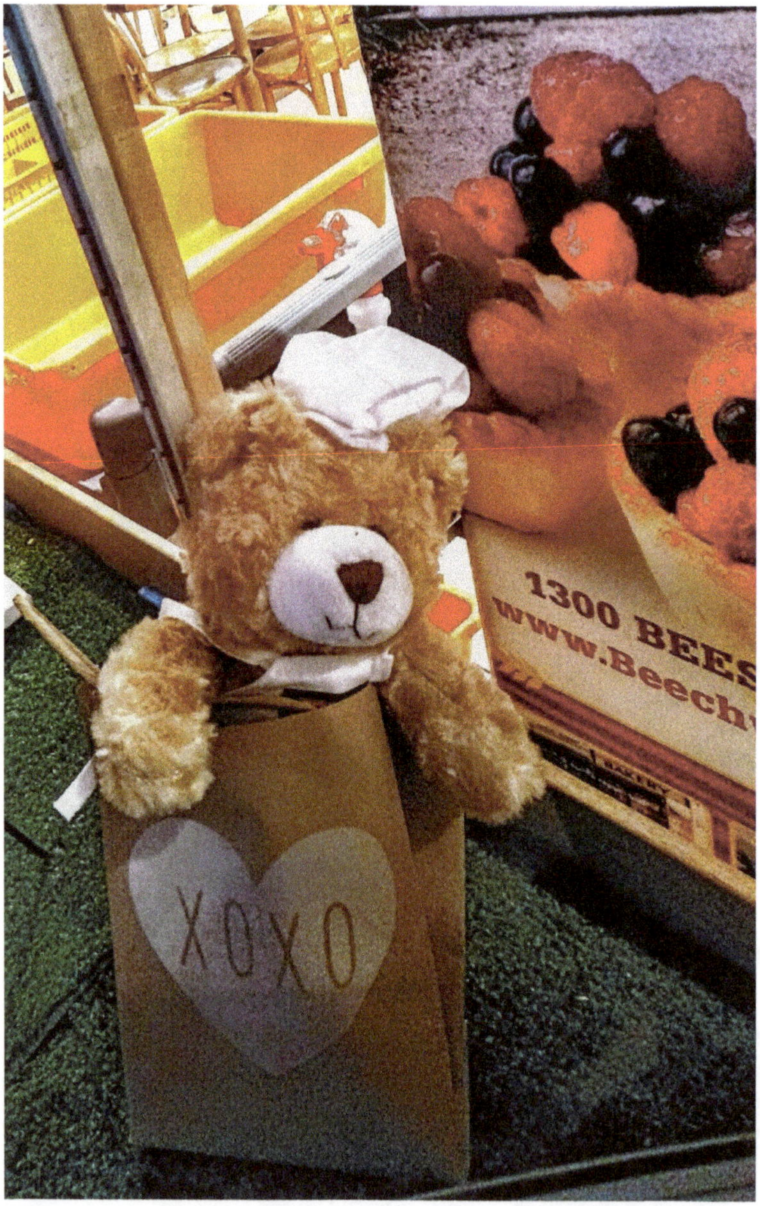
1300 BEES
www.Beech
XOXO

to bear scones

                    I am in
                    an XO carry-bear-bag

                    I'm ready

                    let's go

                                    I can bake
                                        a scone

'm loos

        mumfin' s'appen
          oo m'noz

           'm loos

            ooo

chutney and the condiments

hello visitors

my name
is *chutney*

we are the
acapella
bear band

chutney
and
the *condiments* . . .

bee stung!

oh no
oh no
oh dear

it can't be true

it just can't
be true

don't look

don't listen

don't say
Tom has sold
all of the beestings!

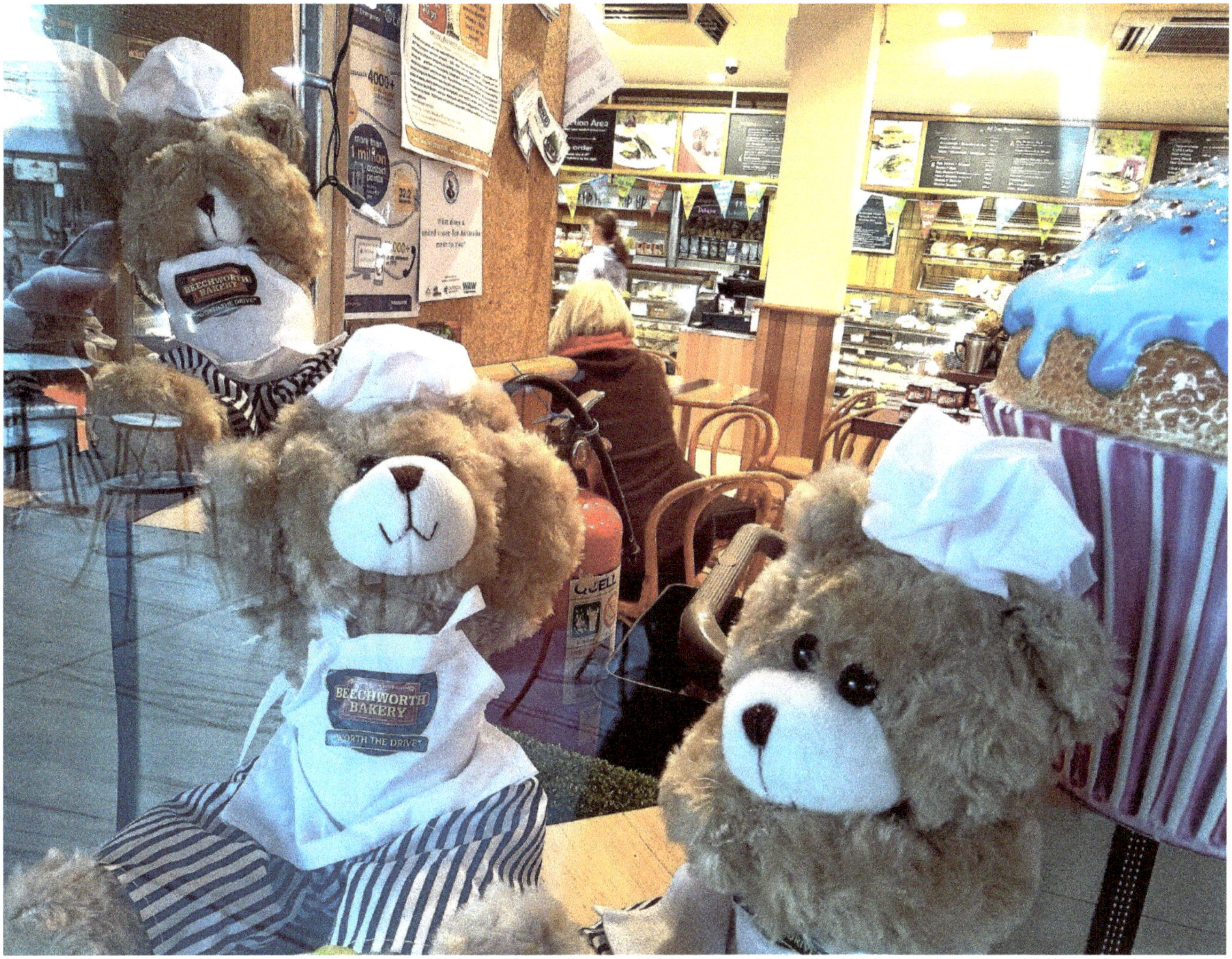
BEECHWORTH BAKERY
"WORTH THE DRIVE"

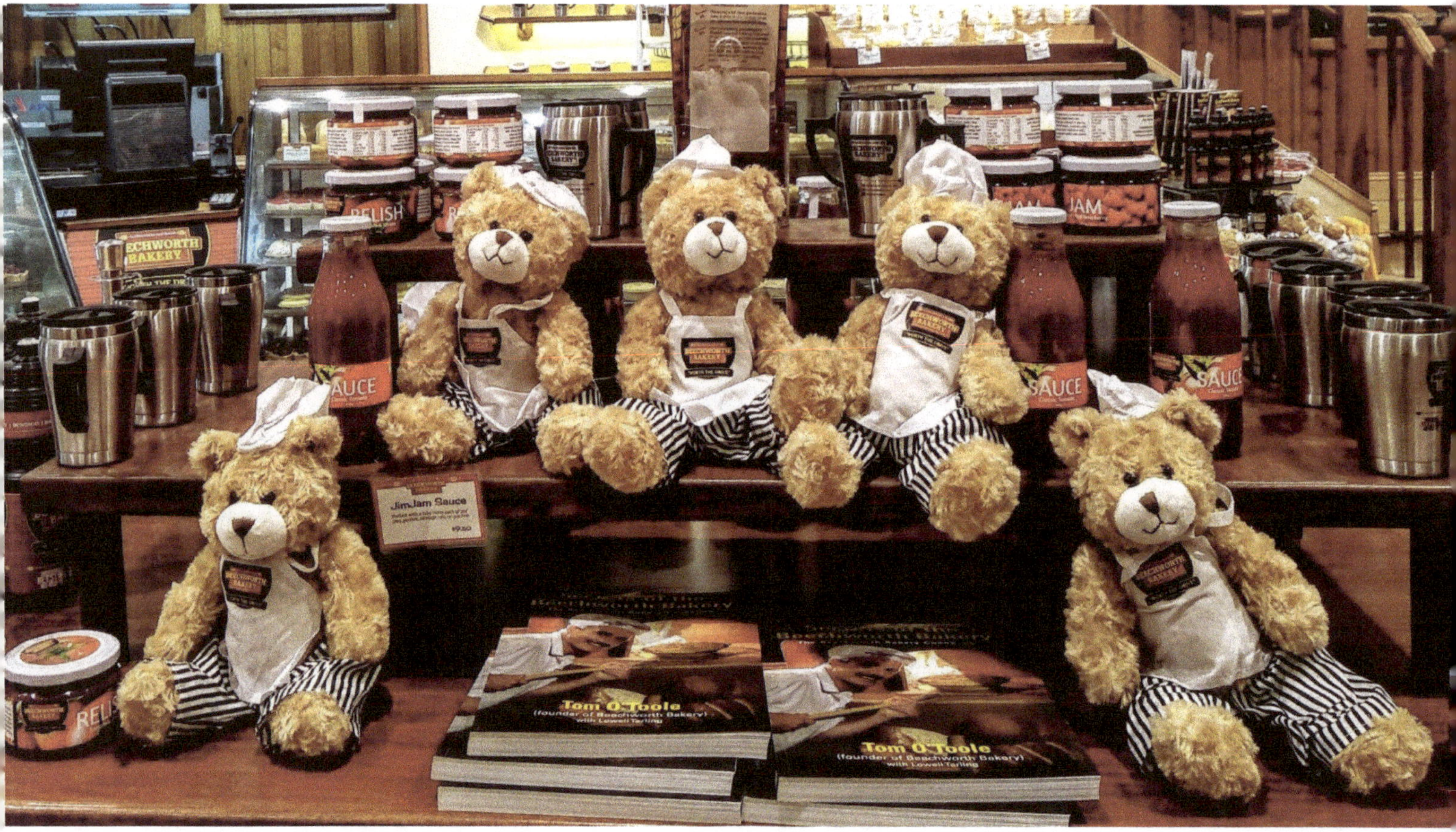
BEECHWORTH BAKERY
RELISH
SAUCE
JAM
JimJam Sauce
$9.50
Tom O'Toole
(founder of Beechworth Bakery)
with Lowell Tarling

bear watch

        sometimes

        we watch

        that is all

        we watch

        we
        can see
        you

            we know
                what you are doing

baker-ee baker sea

boats
out on the ocean

we sail below
the travel cups

we sail around
the red
reusables

sailor bears
we
are sailor bears

on
the baker-sea
in leaky
basket boats

regatta

come on
Ted

if we
stay focused
we can
win

hee hee hee

look at
them

they're all over
the boat!

anyone

isn't anyone
coming?

I will
XOXO
you

anyone?

<sigh>

chillin'

        hi

        I'm just chillin'
        for a minute

        it's been
        a long day

        what about you?

                going alright?

sing along

        one size bears

                one size
                take away

        three size cups

                three size bears

        and three size
        take away

                and one size cups

        come on
        join in

        you can sing
        in the next part

        ready?

button eyed

he's not
really
my brother

we just look
the same

I think
it might be
because
our eyes
are made out of
buttons

it's Olaf

who
is the baker

is it
Olaf?

is it
Tom?

I think
it must be Olaf

Tom is riding a bicycle

that's not
how to bake
bread

(but it looks like excellent fun)

taste test

        excuse me . . .

           excuse me . . .

              ex-*CUSE* me

can you tell me . . . (er hmm!)

us
I mean

can you tell
us

        what does coffee
           taste like?

        is it as nice
           as honey?

me and

Tom said
      to keep an eye
           on you

    are you
        going to get a cake?

I'm watching you

      we're watching you

          me and Tom

at least a labrador

no bear
likes to be
alone

at least
I have some jam

and a plastic labrador
to keep me
company

and a cup
too

and . . .

. . . and stripy pants

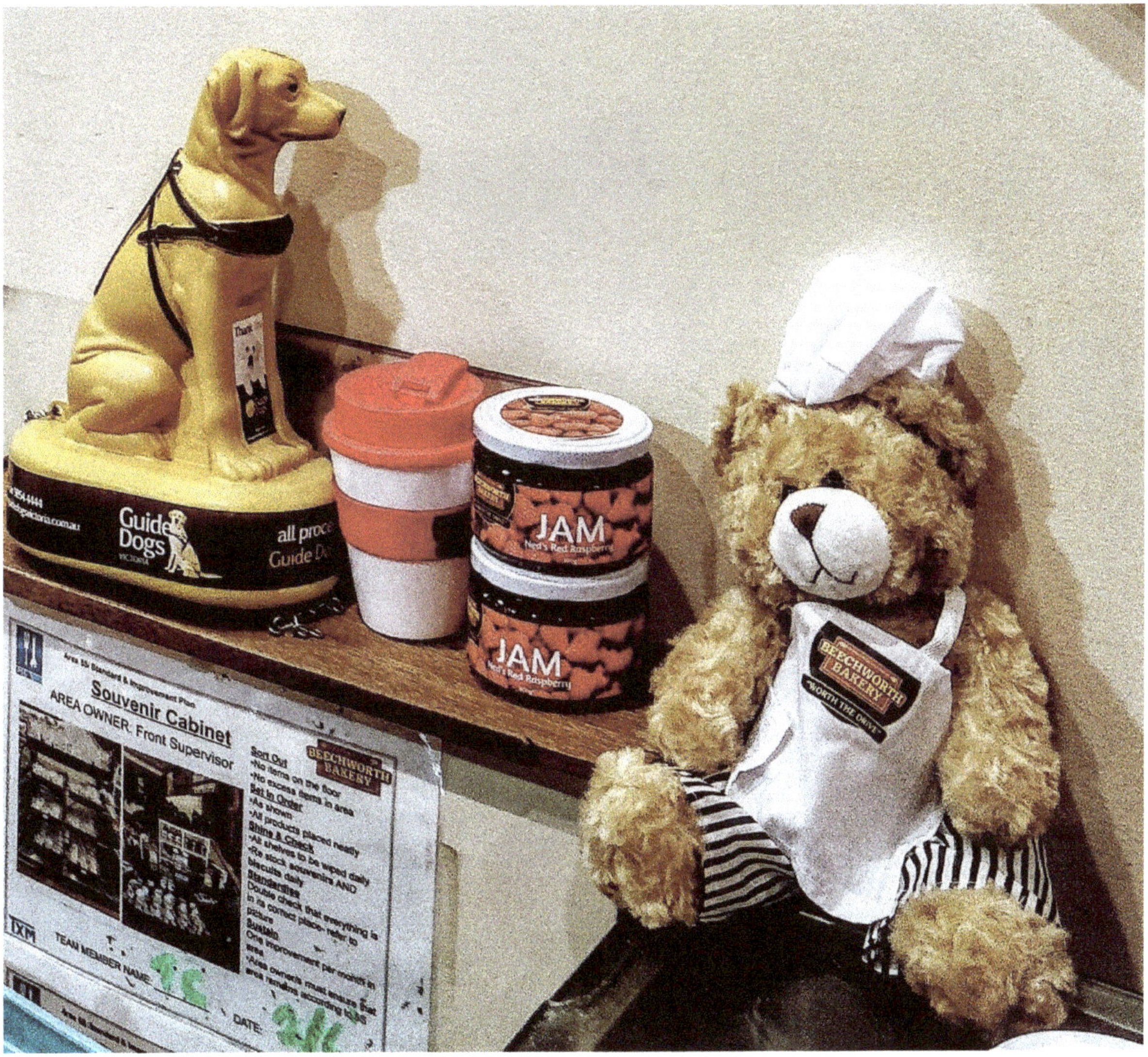
Guide Dogs
JAM
Ned's Red Raspberry
JAM
Ned's Red Raspberry
BEECHWORTH BAKERY
"WORTH THE DRIVE"
Souvenir Cabinet
AREA OWNER: Front Supervisor
BEECHWORTH BAKERY
TEAM MEMBER NAME:
DATE:

the model

        I've got
        a *ha-at*

            I've got
            a *ha-at!*

do you like my hat?

it gets very sunny
in some parts
of the bakery

    very sunny indeed

do you like it?

                I am
              a *hat* model

souvenir

travel mugs
and bakery books

we are the bears
that get
the looks

if you need
a souvenir

don't look elsewhere
because
we
are

here!

down a quart

      come closer . . .

           come closer . . .

              closer . . .

          s-s-s-l-l-l-u-u-u-r-r-r-p-p-p!

your level
is now down
by one quart
of coffee

                (hee hee)

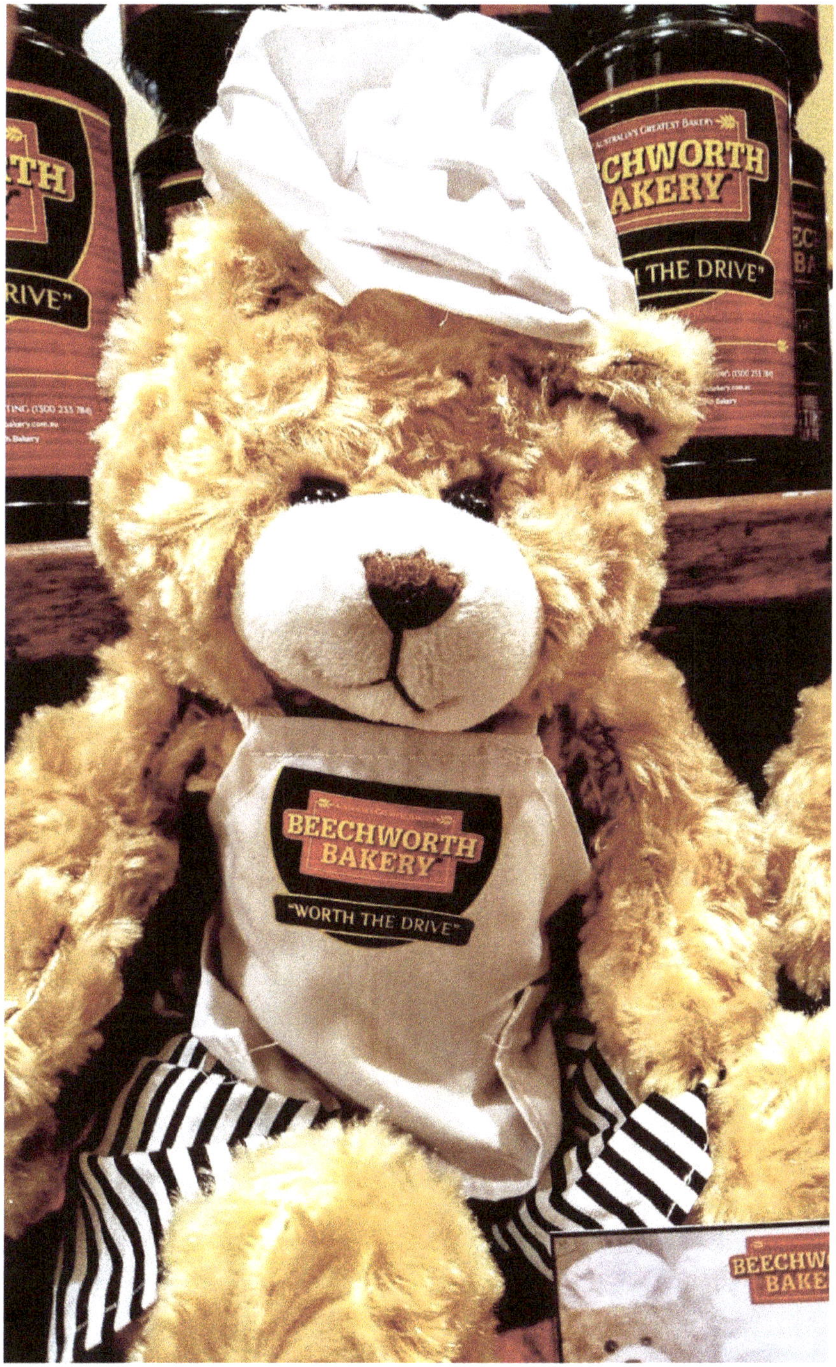
BEECHWORTH
BAKERY
"WORTH THE DRIVE"
CHWORTH
AKERY
H THE DRIVE"

two of us (and . . .)

there used to be
a lot of us

    yes
    but they got sold

there's only us
two
now

    don't forget
    bottom bear

yes yes
it's us two
and bottom bear

(I hope he gets sold
soon)

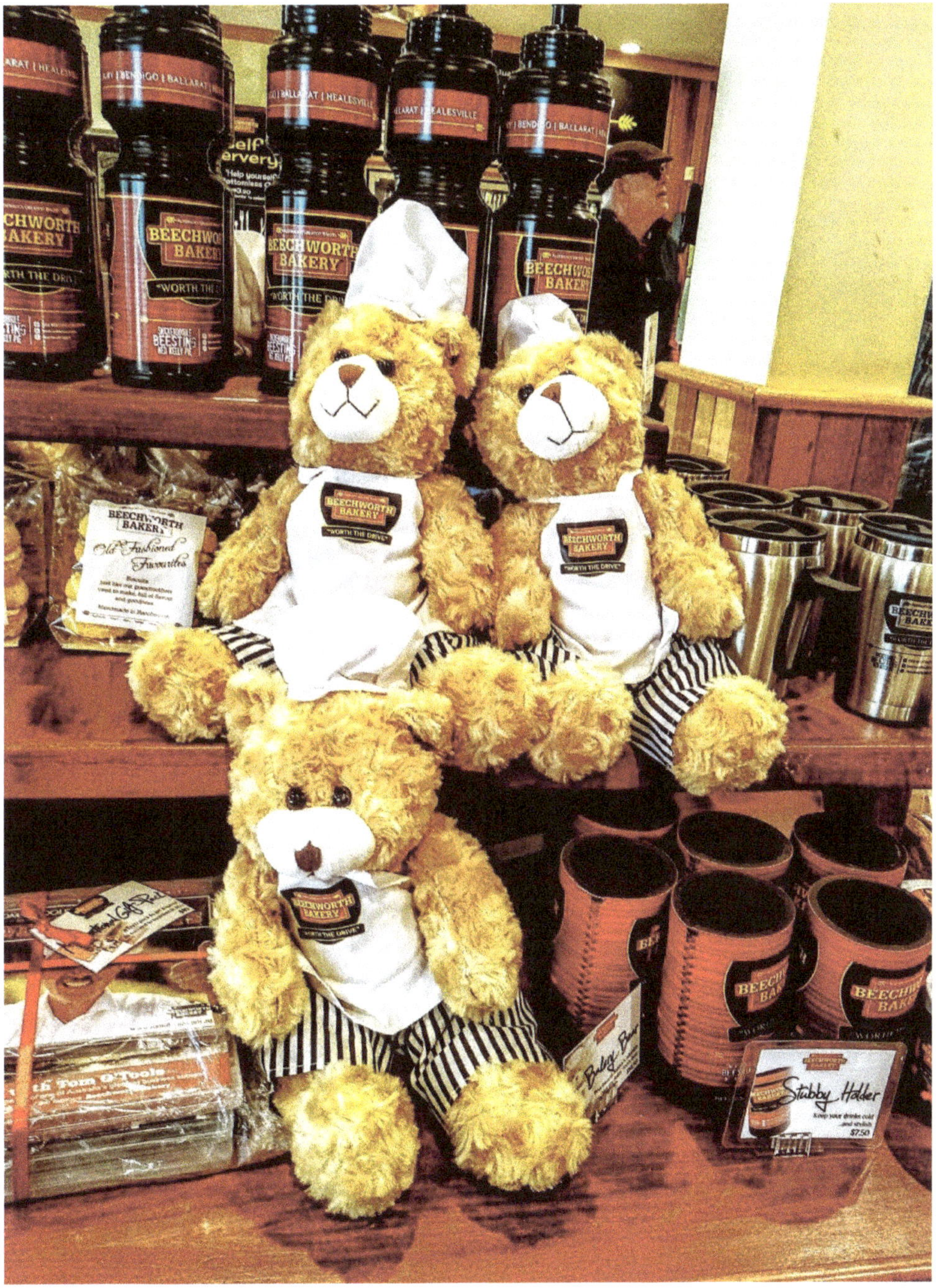
BEECHWORTH BAKERY
"WORTH THE DRIVE"
Old Fashioned Favourites
Stubby Holder
$7.50

a snicker-*WHAT?*

      is that
      a snickerdoodle
      in the cup?

           a *what?*

                <u>what</u>
                <u>do THEY look like?</u>

           oh I see it

           it's written
           up there

ye-es
but . . .

is that
a snickerdoodle
in the cup?

three-bear bobs

        three bear
            bobsled

                in and out
                    of the recycles

                    yeah
                      bear

                watch us
                    g-o—oo-oooo-oooo

tea-party pies

do you think
this
is hidden enough
for our secret
tea party picnic?

will you pour
the tea

I feel like
it's getting
a bit
warm
in here

are you sure
they aren't going to start
to heat
the pies?

more three-bear bobs

and still the bear
bob-sled team
is in the lead

      sliding over the top
      of the slow old
      silver
      travel mugs

            boy
            these bears are
            slick!

oh dear

                                          oh dear

                                             oh
                                            dear

                                          someone
                                     left the honey out
                                         last night

                                             oh
                                           dear

                                             oh
                                           dear

in conclusion

wise bears
three

we inspect

we consider

we
adjudicate

we now conclude that
a biscuit
is needed . . .

. . . and a coffee . . .

. . . before any further
thinking
can take place

About the Author

Frank Prem has been a storytelling poet for over forty years.
When not writing or reading his poetry to an audience, he fills his time by working as a psychiatric nurse.

He has been published in magazines, e-zines and anthologies, in Australia and in a number of other countries, and has both performed and recorded his work as 'spoken word'.

Frank has published numerous collections of free verse poetry, including: *Small Town Kid* (2018), *Devil In The Wind* (2019), and *The New Asylum* (2019) and the three collections that comprise A Love Poetry Trilogy – *Walk Away, Silver Heart* (2020), *A Kiss for the Worthy* (2020), *Rescue and Redemption* (2020) and Pebbles to Poems (2020).

He and his wife live in the beautiful township of Beechworth in northeast Victoria (Australia).

More Picture Poetry by Frank Prem

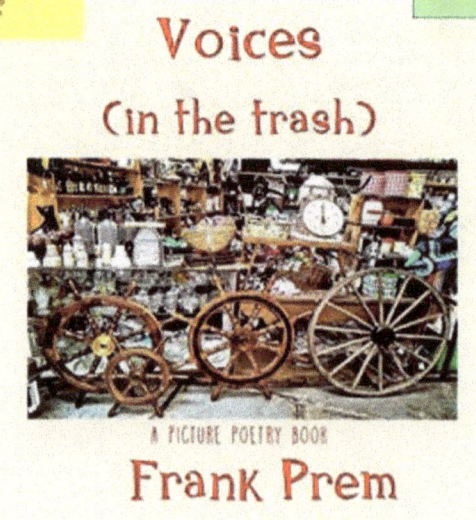

FrankPrem.com

www.ingramcontent.com/pod-product-compliance
Lightning Source LLC
Chambersburg PA
CBHW051254110526
44588CB00026B/2991